ALICE SEIPP

The illustration of the little girls you see above is from the cover of the December 1920 *Inspiration* newsletter that was published by the Woman's Institute of Domestic Arts and Sciences which inspired my book *Vintage Notions*. I chose to update the cover of this edition with more colorful artwork depicting a mother and daughter enjoying the holidays, from the December, 1929 issue of *Fashion Services,* a Woman's Institute Magazine.

Edited by GUSTAVE L. WEINSS

Christmas Morning

BY THE EDITOR

CHRISTMAS MORNING! What greater thrill of delight can we experience than the world alive with rejoicing over the birth of our Saviour—"For unto you is born this day in the city of David a Saviour, which is Christ the Lord."

How our thoughts return to Him who came not to destroy but to save, whose mission it was to spread the message of peace on earth, good-will to man. Now if ever comes the opportunity to renew our faith in Him, and in so doing cast aside our thoughts of self and rejoice with all in the common bond of human brotherhood.

CHRISTMAS MORNING! What other event can set the heart abeating rhythmically to the melody of profound happiness! Well may we sing

> Be merry all, be merry all,
> With holly dress the festive hall;
> Prepare the song, the feast, the ball,
> To welcome Merry Christmas.

The children, after weeks of unusually good behavior and patient waiting, awake from their dreams of a visit from Santa Claus and rush to the Christmas tree to see what their patron saint has brought them. Filled with expectancy, they view their gifts with awe and then gaily enter into the Christmas spirit.

The elders, too, watching the young people, find stealing over them that deep, inexplicable feeling which comes to every one who has been "laboring o' nights" planning for the happiness of others.

CHRISTMAS MORNING! What an inspiration for us to seek out the needy and share with them the prosperity that has been ours!

O delightful Christmas morn, when we can make glad the hearts of those who are saddened and lighten the burdens of those oppressed.

We have around us, wherever we chance to look, those with whom the world has been none too kind —the sick, the poor, the victims of circumstances. Be they grown-ups, let us share with them of our bounty, of our overflowing cup of happiness; be they children, let us help to fulfill their Christmas dreams and brighten their anticipation of the future.

Christmas giving to the needy! How it lightens our cares, how it rewards us in satisfaction, making us bigger, better, broader—more human.

CHRISTMAS MORNING! What brings to us more extreme satisfaction than a visit with our loved ones! Home coming is the thought of those who must labor afar, and while many cannot go home in reality, they can be there in spirit.

Thoughts of home that are and even of homes that were are good for us. Looking back, especially to childhood days, when our trials were softened by loving hearts and hands, prompts us to spread good cheer among friends old and new, awakens in us love for our fellow beings. And, after all, such sentiment is constructive, for it results in good.

CHRISTMAS MORNING! What a wonderful lesson this wondrous morn teaches us. At its coming, we learn more thoroughly the lesson of faith, not only in Him whose birth we celebrate, but in humankind in general. Faith is a force of life without which we could not achieve. It spurs us on and makes possible the seemingly impossible.

We learn to rejoice, not so much at our own deeds, but at the happiness that we have had a part in making possible. Such rejoicing is a tonic for the blues; it points out to us that a little kindness, a little love, expressed or implied, sends forth a shaft of light that brightens souls.

We learn to reflect, and in reflecting we see our own shortcomings; we become filled with a desire to weed out bad traits and encourage good ones.

We learn to share. Thrice blessed is he who, having more than his needs demand, seeks out and shares with those whose wants are many and whose means are few.

CHRISTMAS MORNING! Let the Christmas morning of this year be one that makes us a child again for at least a day, when griefs and sorrows and quarrels change quickly into happiness and gladness and love for all. Let it be one in which gratitude and kindness and good cheer will radiate from us as the light of Christmas radiated from the blazing Yule log in days of yore. Then, when this day of days draws to an end, our hearts will be so filled with the spirit of Christmas that, if my wish to all could be fulfilled, it will remain with us in the days to come and every morning of our lives will be a veritable Christmas morning.

Cooperating With Yourself

By MARY BROOKS PICKEN
Director of Instruction

HAVE you ever stopped to think of the Spirit of Christmas—the jovial, generous feeling that Christmas packages, wreaths, and ribbon give to one, acting as an energy, interest, and enthusiasm tonic?

When I see Christmas big-heartedness, all the little grudges forgotten, and every one thinking of the happiness of some one else, I wish deeply and sincerely that all the year round could be Christmas, when every one starts thinking of some one else and finds joy in abundance throughout the thinking. Planning happy surprises for March as well as December is a profitable thing and brings returns a thousandfold.

A LITTLE while ago I received a letter that pleased and interested me greatly. A precious little lady out West wrote like this:

"I am thirty-five; have three children. The older two are girls. There is a dancing class in our town and the parents can go and take lessons at the same time the children have their lessons. So I coaxed my husband and we went, and we have gone every week for some time.

"As I have gone, I have realized that dresses are shorter and more girlish, and—well, now comes the story. I shortened my dresses, combed my hair a fluffy, becoming way, and bought some real nice face powder; and as I have seen the pretty things that other girls wear, I have made or bought similar things for myself, and truly my husband and I have been closer together than at any time since our first baby. We visit so much more and I know he is proud of me, and now I find myself dressing up to surprise and delight him, not freshening up just because it is time for him to come home. Dan actually says I am ten years younger and that I dance with him better than any other girl in the class.

"But now here is the trouble. My mother and my older sister are horrified. My shorter skirts, new hair dress, and powder have actually caused demoralization in their eyes, and I don't know what to do about it. They say that every one will say that Dan's wife is fickle and cares only for dress, and I really don't want them to feel that way about me. Sometimes I think maybe I have gone to the extreme about things, but it has been such fun being young and happy again, and feeling as if I were truly Dan's sweetheart. Mother says that after fourteen years of married life I should get over such silliness, but it doesn't seem silly to me. It seems like living life

in real earnest and having a good time meanwhile."

To me, this was a wonderful letter. I just felt as if I should like every one to read it. Why should one hesitate to be happy, to live fully? If it takes shorter skirts, powder, and a new way of doing the hair to turn the corner into Youth's high-

---

---

way, I say greet them as blessings and rejoice that they are within the reach of every one.

OFTEN we hear that men are just boys grown big, that they are at heart always boys. Women often realize this with their own men folk, but instead of being young, happy girls, they allow their mother instinct to dominate and proceed to mother their husbands just as they do their children. Then comes the danger of losing the sentiment of youth, a breach is unconsciously begun and makes a place for itself.

Christmas, when all the tenderness in the human heart is awake, oftentimes offers opportunity to bridge such breaks, to dissolve wordlessly any misunderstandings, and to bring loved ones close, and especially through a greater appreciation of true comradeship.

AS I read letters from those I serve through Woman's Institute work, the greater my appreciation for womankind

becomes. The courage and sheer pluck evidenced by so many delight me. My training and concentration have always been along domestic lines, and I have preached economy, thrift, good housekeeping. I believe in them because in working with them I know their virtues. But even I insist that it is more creditable to be a homemaker than a housekeeper. It is better to make hastily a smart, becoming frock than a perfect dress that must be worn two or three seasons because of the labor involved in the making. Even I say that a sausage-and-waffle supper is better than one that requires a whole afternoon's preparation if in making the afternoon kind a chance to play is sacrificed.

Play makes for better work and easier work, for, in reality, healthy playing is cooperating with oneself toward a better expression of life, love, and Christianity.

COOPERATING with oneself in a worthy cause is practical and satisfying, and it is a glorious thing to do when it is about something that touches the depths of one's heart, brings light to the eyes and buoyancy to the step. The Christmas Spirit does that for us; it exhilarates and inspires, for in making Christmas one must romp again on Youth's highway. When you take hold of Christmas this year, put the Spirit of Christmas into your heart deep and secure. Dress up for Christmas, be young, cheery, and gay, and make all your family and friends glad that you know how to cooperate with yourself and them in making the best of every day.

Last-Minute Christmas Suggestions

By ALWILDA FELLOWS
Department of Dressmaking

IN SPITE of the good resolutions made in regard to preparing for Christmas during October and November, December finds many anticipations of the average person unrealized, the inevitable pressure of holiday work making itself more forceful and perhaps more difficult each day. Time and expense, two factors that influence so many of our plans and activities, seem to have a special significance around the Christmas season, and as this draws nearer the solution of the gift problem usually resolves itself into the making of some inexpensive article not requiring a great deal of time.

BABIES, for some reason or other, always head the Christmas-gift list, but often this primary consideration given them does little more than add a rattle-box or two to their already overburdened collection. This year, why not delight some mother with an abundant supply of bonnet strings for the tiniest member of her family? The bonnet string at the left is of lawn finished with a hand hem-stitched hem and an edging of fine tatting. The string in the center is of batiste, the lower portion being a pin-tucked section trimmed with lace and insertion. Linen of very fine weave, scalloped in white with an extra row of buttonhole stitches in blue and tiny embroidery flowers of white, pink, and blue makes the string at the right very interesting.

Rosettes, too, have real utility value. These may be made of ¼- to ½-inch pink and blue double-faced ribbon, each loop knotted in the center, as at the upper left.

AT THE upper center is shown a card-table cover made of a 30-inch square of imitation linen having the corners cut as illustrated. In one corner a cross-stitch basket design is worked in various colors, tan predominating. The edge is finished with a narrow hem secured with the twisted running-stitch in tan and green.

CONSIDERABLE latitude is permitted in the choice of materials for luncheon sets, Japanese crêpe in soft colors being one of the recent novelties. A cloth as well as the napkins shown at the upper right, if made of fine Japanese crêpe and trimmed with a needle picot edge and an initial of contrasting color, would be very pleasing. To make the edge, first turn a narrow hem, and then, using very soft floss, take blanket-stitches over the hem to secure it. Make the blanket-stitches almost ¼ inch apart, and after completing every fourth stitch, insert the needle in the edge of the material, as shown in the detail illustration, wind the thread around the needle a considerable number of times, and draw the thread up tight to form the picot effect.

HANDKERCHIEFS similar to those shown at the right are made of white or colored linen or fine batiste and embroidered in tiny motifs of contrasting color. One thread of soft strand floss should be used for the embroidery in order to make it very dainty. The border effect is formed by drawing threads of the material and inserting floss of contrasting color in their place. To do this, at the point desired, draw a thread of the material. Then skip one thread and draw another thread. To the end of the thread that is left, tie a couple of strands of floss; then very carefully draw out the linen thread, taking hold of the opposite end. The contrasting thread tied to this will be drawn through as the linen thread is taken out.

PLAIN or figured material of sheer cotton or light-weight silk is suitable for the negligée or boudoir jacket shown at the lower center. To make this negligée, crease a full width of material 1¼ to 1⅜ yards long lengthwise, as at *a* in the diagram, and crosswise, as at *b*, through the center. To provide the neck opening, make a downward slash 7 or 8 inches long on the lengthwise crease from the intersection of the creases made in the material, as at *c*; then slash on slightly diagonal lines upwards from this same point *c*, as at *d*, on both sides of the lengthwise crease, making these slashes 2½ or 3 inches long. Form three triangular-shaped trimming portions by folding the corners back on lines connecting the terminations of the slashes, at at *e*. At *f* is shown one revers-like portion turned back and at *g* the back collar portion that is formed.

The neck and revers edges may be finished with picoting or narrow bindings, or the turned-back portions may be faced with either plain or figured fabric. No seams are required in this jacket. The edges of the material may be finished as desired, the jacket slipped over the head, and the underarm edges tied together with ribbons.

Cheer in the Christmas Feast

By LAURA MacFARLANE
Editorial Department

SURELY no better word could be found to describe the Christmas season than the one that is used—Merry. Though this holiday is usually attended by cold, bleak winds and an abundance of snow, everything seems to lend a hand in making it the merriest festival of the year. It does not take one long to fall into the spirit of the occasion once the preparations begin. The house becomes aglow with wreaths of holly, sprays of mistletoe, and patches of brilliant red here and there, which, with the aroma of the pine, the gleam of the bayberry candles, and the glow from the burning Yule log awaken the household to the realization that it is time to welcome Merry Christmas.

But while we are getting our homes in holiday attire and filling ourselves with the Christmas spirit, we must not overlook the Christmas feast. This should play a very important part in the Yuletide preparations if the holidays are to be a season of joy for all. Although the housewife tries to do her best in the culinary art all the year around, she makes a special effort at Christmas time, preparing the dainties and delicacies that she may consider almost prohibitive at any other season.

A menu for the Christmas dinner is suggested here that may be adopted in its entirety or changed to suit one's preference. Roast duck or chicken can very well take the place of turkey or a fine crown roast of pork served with apples would make a splendid substitute.

FOR the first course, fruit cocktail is suggested because it is such a splendid appetizer and because fruit is not included elsewhere in the menu. This may be a combination of fruits such as oranges, grapefruit, malaga grapes, pineapple, and white cherries, or it may be grapefruit served attractively with maraschino cherries. A sprig of holly dresses up considerably the small plate on which the cocktail glass or grapefruit shell is served.

If you were forehanded enough to can some of the excellent green corn in which your garden or the market abounded in September, take one of your cans from the shelf and use it for your Christmas dinner. One woman whose family is fond of this vegetable always puts up several cans of the small, tender ears of golden bantam corn and then uses these for all her special dinners during the winter. Corn that has been removed from the ear and then canned makes excellent corn soufflé or corn fritters for such meals.

In the way of salad, nothing is more appropriate for this very special dinner than poinsettia salad served with Thousand Island dressing. On some crisp lettuce leaves, arrange pieces of beet or tomato to resemble the petals of the poinsettia flower. Fill the center with the yolk of a hard-cooked egg put through a ricer. Have a dish of Thousand Island dressing on the table and let each person take the desired amount.

Christmas Dinner Menu

Fruit Cocktail

Cream of Asparagus Soup   Croutons

Celery   Olives

Roast Turkey   Oyster Stuffing

Brown Gravy   Cranberry Jelly

Browned Sweet Potatoes   Corn

Mashed Turnips

Poinsettia Salad   Thousand Island Dressing

Plum Pudding   Hard Sauce

Nuts   Raisins   Candies

Coffee

ALTHOUGH plum pudding seems a rather heavy dessert for the menu usually chosen for Christmas, the meal proves woefully lacking if it is not topped off by a rich steaming pudding served with a light, creamy hard sauce. As far back as we can remember, we recall the joy we experienced when we caught sight of the pudding being brought from the kitchen with such ceremony. The following recipe makes a pudding large enough to serve twelve persons:

CHRISTMAS PUDDING

2½ c. stale bread crumbs	⅓ c. chopped citron
½ c. milk	½ c. chopped nuts
1 c. beef suet	1 c. flour
½ c. sugar	½ tsp. soda
½ c. molasses	1 tsp. baking powder
2 eggs	1 tsp. salt
1 c. chopped raisins	⅓ c. fruit juice

Soak the bread crumbs in the milk. Work the suet with the hands until it is creamy, and to it add the sugar, molasses, and well-beaten eggs. Mix with the milk and bread crumbs, and add the fruit and nuts. Mix the dry ingredients and sift them into the mixture. Add the fruit juice, turn into a buttered mold, and steam 3 hours. Serve hot with hard sauce.

HARD SAUCE

⅓ c. butter	1 egg white
1 c. powdered sugar	⅜ tsp. vanilla

Cream the butter, add the sugar gradually, and then fold in the egg white beaten stiff. Add the vanilla and beat until light and creamy. A very attractive way to serve plum pudding is to place it on the center of a good-sized platter and then have individual servings of hard sauce in small crinkled paper cases arranged around the pudding. One of these may be placed on each person's plate of pudding.

Speaking of plum pudding, have you ever used it for Christmas gifts? It can be steamed in small-sized molds, such as baking powder cans or little bowls, and then tied up attractively and sent to some friend who will appreciate this bit of home cookery. Wrap the pudding first in oiled paper, then in tin foil, and lastly in a square of red crêpe paper. Gather the paper together at the top, tie with red ribbon to which a card can be attached, and insert a sprig of holly.

SO FAR as confections for the holiday season are concerned, there is a large variety from which to choose. Glacé nuts and fruits, fondant candies, stuffed prunes, dates, and figs, chocolate-coated nuts, and similar dainties always please the grown-ups, while peanut brittle, popcorn balls, caramels, cracker jack, fudge, penuchie, taffy, and lollypops are especially appealing to the younger generation. And if a children's party is being planned for the holidays, no more attractive favor can be chosen than lollypops dressed up fantastically in red crêpe paper to resemble dolls. The candy part should be used for the face on which eyes, nose, and mouth are marked. A gay hat and a flying scarf complete the costume.

Fig and marshmallow figures are bound to please the eye of the child. These are fashioned on two nails that are driven through a small wooden standard. Raisins are used for the legs; almonds stuck with a glacé sirup for the feet; figs for the skirt or short trousers; a plump fig for the body; a marshmallow having features marked with melted chocolate for the head; currants strung on wires for the arms; peanuts for the hands; and a fig for the cap.

Youthful Hair Decorations

By MARY MAHON
Department of Millinery

SEEKING the beautiful in color and form is the basic instinct of human nature, and style in dress is one of the essentials in the joy of living. This joy is evident in the tiny tot when she views herself in the mirror after mother has dressed her up and added a new or different ribbon to her hair or dress. Her pleasure and delight just radiate, showing that from the youngest miss to the smart, alert girl of fourteen the ribbon bow means a world of pleasure. Thus we see that from childhood it is very difficult for any of us to resist appearance. We really enjoy our own possession of anything pretty, and while we sometimes hate to confess it, we like display. Some of us enjoy others' appreciation even more.

CHILDREN, in particular, love to imitate the grown-up sister and mother. Designers in hats and dresses are making exact reproductions of the grown-ups' models in juvenile clothes, and this is also true of head-dresses.

For artistic effect, fashion at present demands that with every dinner and evening gown an appropriate head-dress or comb be worn. Since these ornate arrangements mean so much to the young girl, it would surely delight her heart to receive one for a Christmas gift, for there are so many opportunities to wear them during the festive season.

THE accompanying illustrations serve to show a few of the season's favorite head-dresses that are very much worn. You will note that even the extreme and fanciful arrangements of the debutante are imitated in little sister's hair band. A decidedly new note is struck in the bronze leaves used in a flat wreath in Fig. 1, which is studded with rhinestones or any gay colored beads. Gold cloth is used to make a similar hair band for little sister, as shown in Fig. 1A. Numerous daisy petals are made of the gold cloth to form the wreath, which is finished at the ear with two hand-made daisies having centers of bright-colored beads. This arrangement can also be made of any colored silk that would match her sash.

NEXT, in Fig. 2A we have a dainty, wee miss of six who is wishing with all her heart that big sister would have a debut every day so that she could wear a pretty ribbon fashioned after sister's coiffure band with an opalescent butterfly and aigrette, as shown in Fig. 2.

The ever popular Grecian band of silver ribbon, shown in Fig. 3, with small hand-made silk flowers in pastel coloring combined with tiny pearl beads appliquéd directly in front is especially pretty and can be worn with almost any color gown. This particular style with a loose bow knotted at the back, as in Fig. 3A, is very appropriate for the miss who has not yet turned up her pretty curls, but feels truly grown up when she dons her party frock.

Woman's Institute *Question Box*

Spring Fabrics and Colors

Has any definite decision in regard to spring fabrics been made as yet? I would certainly appreciate information in regard to fabrics and also colors that will probably be featured.
G. E. S.

A number of showings of spring ready-to-wear lines have already been held. Continuance of twilled and ribbed woolen materials of various kinds is evident in these models, tricotine still being a prominent feature and a fine quality of rep coming into favor. These early showings do not place any emphasis on serge, however. Tweeds and homespuns are featured by some of the better houses, covert cloth is shown to some extent, and velour, especially in conservative checks, is evident.

It is said that the majority of separate skirts for spring will be of wool rather than silk. For sports wear, white is very promising, flannel being especially good and serge and broadcloth coming second.

Rather heavy weaves of crêpe will undoubtedly head the silk fabrics, although taffeta for youthful models will be given decided prominence. Many of the crêpe weaves have fine stripes, small plaids, or little old-fashioned flowers. Crêpe de Chine and satin weaves are bound to remain in favor for the models that retain the present silhouette, but with the return of wider skirts, stiffer silks are inevitable. For instance, heavy moiré silk has already made its appearance.

As to colors, navy and black in dresses seem to have dominance over other colors for early spring wear. The French color card shows many brilliant and warm colors, but these are intended chiefly for decorative purposes.

A series of browns and grays, ranging from light to dark shades, may be included as principal colors along with navy and black, and judging from the many delightful, bright colors shown in the textile color card made in the United States, for later spring wear we shall not need to be at all conservative in our selection of the colors we like most. This card shows a number of true blues in medium and dark shades and slightly greenish blues in light tones. In addition, spring greens in light and dark tones, a range of orange from Honeydew, a light melon color, to pimento, which has a decided reddish cast, a wide assortment of tans and browns, some with henna influence, grays in light and dark tones, and a touch of red and violet make up a very attractive display.

Want to Get Acquainted?

The following Institute students desire to become acquainted with other Institute students residing in their localities:

I should like to meet some young married woman, between the ages of 20 and 40 years, who resides in Los Angeles and is taking the Dressmaking and Tailoring Course. B. L.

I should like to become acquainted with students of the Woman's Institute. MISS MURIEL MONTGOMERY, Faulkner Co., Vilonia, Ark.

I should like to become acquainted with students about 19 years of age. J. McM.

I am interested in getting a position in a dressmaker's shop in Des Moines, Iowa. L. S.

(Continued at bottom of next page)

Christmas Baskets

THE charming custom of dropping May baskets on the doorsteps of one's friends on May day may be the inspiration for the sending of baskets at Christmas time. At any rate, the custom has become quite prevalent, and well it may, for a gift of this kind usually brings much joy to both the one who prepares it and the one who receives it. There is really a splendid variety in basket gifts, for, while they always include food of some kind, they give, as shown here, the sender an opportunity to carry out any original ideas she may have in both the contents and the decorations.

MANY persons are in the habit of sending Christmas dinners to those who are a little less fortunate than they, but often they give very little thought to the way in which they send the food. A gift of this kind will be much more appreciated if it is arranged neatly and attractively in a large, substantial market basket, as shown in the center, and it will carry with it much more of the Christmas spirit if it is decorated with holly, bitter sweet, a spray of evergreen, or a real Christmassy potted plant.

THE girl or woman who is an adept at home-made candies and cookies will find that her gifts are very popular, especially if she packs them artistically, in a somewhat unusual basket. Take, for instance, the round or the heart-shaped basket on the right. Baskets of this kind are very inexpensive when they are purchased in the natural color and then colored and trimmed at home according to one's fancy. Any good stain of the desired color may be used. A Chinese ring and tassel and large jade beads, which any art store can supply, give the round basket a real Oriental touch. The conventional rose design on the heart-shaped basket may be done in wool or raffia or may be stenciled on.

THE square baskets on the left are somewhat of an innovation with their charming ribbon trimmings. Ribbon of good width may be used rather lavishly to tie up such a box after it is packed and may complete the trimmings with a good-sized bow on top; or, narrow ribbon may be interlaced through openings in the top and sides and the top trimmed with several flat loops of ribbon and two or three small ribbon roses and leaves. The little roses may be in different colors, such as blue, yellow, pink, and orchid, so long as the ones chosen harmonize well. Still another variety of trimming is shown on the round basket. Ribbon about 1 inch wide is employed here and both the loops and the ends are knotted.

HAVE you a friend who has been ill for some time and yet is able to enjoy a few simple delicacies? For her, procure an open basket with a handle and in it place several small glasses of a variety of jellies, marmalades, and conserves. Fill in the spaces with such things as sweet chocolates wrapped in tinfoil, tea balls made by wrapping in tinfoil enough of her favorite tea for one brewing, and similar dainties. She may even enjoy a small square of fruit cake tied up in oiled paper. If the basket is large enough, some very fine fruit may be included. The handle can be dressed up by tying to it a bunch or two of candy grapes made by wrapping round, hard candies in oiled paper and joining a number of these by means of fine cord wire to resemble a bunch of grapes.

I should like to become acquainted with students taking the Complete Dressmaking Course who are about 23 years of age and live in or near Farmer's City, Ill. E. C. M.

I should like to become acquainted with Institute students about 13 years of age. L. C.

I should like to correspond with students between 18 and 20 years of age, living in Minnesota, South Dakota, or Iowa. N. C.

I should like to become acquainted with students or graduates of the Woman's Institute who are in business in Los Angeles, Calif. N. I. J.

I should be delighted to hear from any young girls or "old" girls who have young hearts. L. M. D.

I should like to correspond with a lady who has taken, or who is taking, the Millinery Course and who is in business or intends going into business for herself early next year in Portland, Oregon. M. E.

I should like to become acquainted with students between the ages of 20 and 23. X.

I should like to have you publish in INSPIRATION my telephone number, Main 810, and should like to have other San Diego, California, students who wish to become acquainted call me up. H. V.

I should like to communicate with other Woman's Institute students in Africa. M. E. P., South Africa

I should like to become acquainted with New Jersey students about 20 years of age. I. E.

If other Woman's Institute students would like to get in touch with any inquiring students whose name and address are not given, we shall be glad to supply the information.

Circular Skirts

I have heard rumors about the return of circular skirts. Have these rumors any foundation? B. R.

Such rumors are well founded, for circular skirts are being not only shown but in some cases worn by the leaders of fashion. For more than two years an effort has been made by a few designers to bring the circular skirt into prominence, but the straight skirt has proved itself so practical and so well liked universally that women have remained firm in their preference of this model over the flared lines. Circular effects, however, are gaining impetus, for a great many taffeta models for present wear, as well as for spring, are made with long-waisted tight bodices and full circular skirts. In woolen fabrics, also, the circular effect is often seen. This has gone so far as to eliminate fulness at the waist line, thus making the flare more prominent.

Not all designers, however, have sanctioned circular skirts, and there is still a loophole for their postponement in popular favor. But with the price of fabrics declining it is to be assumed that manufacturers will not be averse to backing the movement for fuller skirts, as a few of them have already done, and with the influence that ready-to-wear usually exerts, the circular skirt may before long launch a decided change in silhouette.

Russian Dressing

Kindly send me a recipe for Russian dressing, which is used so much on salads at the present time. E. H. W.

RUSSIAN DRESSING

⅔ c. mayonnaise	½ Tb. scraped onion
1 chopped pimiento or	4 Tb. chilli sauce
½ chopped green pepper	1½ tsp. piccalilli

Into the mayonnaise stir the chopped pimiento or green pepper, the onion, the chilli sauce, and the piccalilli. Chill and serve.

This is quite similar to Thousand Island dressing, except that the piccalilli is omitted and chopped hard-cooked egg used. The mayonnaise used for these dressings may be the cooked or the uncooked variety.

Fashion-Help Inquiries

Very often students wish to make an inquiry concerning a fashion help that we have given them or a design that they have seen in some fashion magazine. In such cases care should be taken to inform us of the number of the pattern, as well as the publication in which it was shown. If this plan is followed, it will enable us to give much better service, for with the many inquiries we receive, there is always a possibility of delay unless we receive this detailed information.

Our Students' *Own Page*

Husband is Proud of Her Ability

I am going to tell you how proud my husband and I are that I took the Course. I make his shirts now and he is so pleased with them that he is showing them to our friends and telling them, "You can't buy any in town like these." I have made my little girls some of the sweetest school dresses as well as dresses, skirts, and waists for myself. I also made my winter coat and my friends all seem to envy me. They hardly believe it when I tell them, because they say to me, "Why, you didn't use to sew at all." One friend said, "You could not make your first baby's clothes." I tell them I know it and that I give all the credit for my success to the Woman's Institute.
Mrs. J. F. Barkell,
R. 3, Box 122, Tacoma, Wash.

Dainty Garments for the Little Visitor

My little layette is progressing very nicely, and I find the greatest enjoyment in working with those tiny garments. By following the instructions in my lesson, they are so easy to make that it takes me only about half the time to complete a little garment that I had thought it would take. I have visited the most exclusive shops and copied their most expensive imported things for a wee per cent. of their cost in the shop. For instance, one little dress with hand-run tucks, a tiny spray of embroidery, and scalloped lower edge finished with lace was marked $25. I copied it in even nicer material for about $3. I know, too, that my little one will have as fine dainty garments as the wealthiest child, and besides the great difference in cost I have had the joy of making them myself.
Mrs. Kathleen Bird,
Box 553, Miami, Okla.

One Season's Dresses for Barely Fifty Dollars

I've been preparing my wardrobe for the winter season and the results certainly are satisfactory. With the dress form, a picture, and almost anything in the way of material, there is no limit to what can be done. My "masterpiece" was made out of

an old velvet coat, a velvet dress, an evening cape, and the trimming from a winter dress. Everybody says it looks like a hundred-dollar dress, but it really cost only for the thread.

I have now made five pretty dresses, and one that I made about a month ago was mistaken for an imported gown. Really, I can't tell you what fun it has been, and it all started because your lessons truly aroused the love of sewing in me.

Just think of having a wardrobe of lovely dresses after having spent barely fifty dollars! Counting in the cost of the lessons, my clothes have cost less this year than ever before. I thank you!
Miss Clorinda B. Ramsey,
Maison Francaise, Middlebury, Vt.

Many Pretty Hats at Very Substantial Savings

I am getting much pleasure out of my Course. I have made twenty-three hats and trimmed four since I began the Course in January, and am not in business either. I have just finished one that would sell for $20 and it cost me only $1.80. Can you beat that? You may say, "Well, you had the material." Surely, but it was in scraps of velvet, satin, and velvet ribbon. Still I made the hat and it is a stylish one, too.
Mrs. D. J. Young,
Canadian, Texas

Having Splendid Success With Shop of Her Own

I feel so deeply how greatly your Course helped me to a speedy success.

My little daughter is too young for me to open a larger shop for a couple of years at least, and so I have had to be content with the two large rooms I can spare from my apartment. Even so, I have kept three girls busy, besides putting out all my embroidery, and we turned out between September 1 and June 31, over one hundred and sixty gowns.

I do not take any morning dresses or odd skirts—just afternoon and evening dresses. Of course, I can ask a good price for this work. I feel that I am doing remarkably well and so far have not had one whom I was unable to please.

After my daughter goes away to school, I hope to grow very rapidly and have a specialty shop just for the making of evening clothes, with which I have had exceptional success. There is undoubtedly greater financial returns from the making of evening clothes and it takes only about one-third as long, I find, to complete a gown. I charge rather stiff prices, but supervise personally, and I am yet to have a complaint on that score. Considering that I can give the public only two to four hours each day, I feel that I have been very successful, and I have turned away a great many customers because I prefer not to take more than can be properly done.
Mrs. Beatrice L. Brennan,
845 Main St., Worcester, Mass.

Takes First Prize at Minnesota State Fair

I must tell you that I entered a little dress at the Minnesota State Fair and it took the first prize in its lot as well as the sweepstake of all the children's dresses entered. I felt quite proud of my work. I wish you could see the dress; it is very pretty. My score was 95 per cent. Also I won first prize on a practical petticoat made after your first drafting lesson.
Mrs. Wm. Carlson,
2613 18th Avenue, South,
Minneapolis, Minn.

Fine Success After Seven Lessons

I am having wonderful success. After completing seven lessons, I copied a voile dress from a magazine for which I made my own pattern, also a waist, and I just finished a pongee blouse, for which I designed and drafted my patterns, and if I do say so, it is the prettiest blouse I have seen this year.

One thing I can say is that no one else has dresses like mine, for I can take all the parts of different blouses or dresses I like and combine them in one blouse or dress.

My husband says I have more than paid for my Course now, for I have made countless things for the kiddies this summer besides my own clothes. My linen dress you were so kind in helping me with was a big success.
Mrs. Herbert Seavy,
Box 12, East Machias, Me.

Has Learned Value of Carefulness in Details

I made my baby a winter coat, and it is really the first thing that has gone together without ripping and fussing. I give my first lesson credit for this, as from it I learned exactness, carefulness, and neatness. I pinned the pattern carefully to the goods and paid attention to all the markings, notches, gather marks, etc., something I have never done because I thought I knew enough about sewing after 10 years of practical experience not to have to bother with the minor details. My clothes always looked pretty good at a distance, but would never bear close inspection.
Mrs. Robert Gastmeyer,
132 Barclay Street,
Flushing, L. I., N. Y.

Saved $14.86 on One Hat

I made myself a pretty hat a couple of weeks ago. I could not afford the only hat I really cared for, so I bought my frame and material and came home. Next morning I had a hat, with better cloring for me than the one I copied and I saved myself $14.86. Besides, I have the satisfaction of not seeing the same kind of hat every time I go out.
Lulah L. Byrns,
2555 Kenilworth Road,
Cleveland, Ohio

ℱashion Service

— SUPPLEMENT —

Each Issue of *Vintage Notions Monthly* includes a *Fashion Service Supplement*. You will read about the fashion styles popular in the early twentieth century and receive a collectible fashion illustration to print and frame.

The students of the Woman's Institute would also receive a publication called *Fashion Service*. Where the *Inspiration* newsletter instructed them on all aspects of the domestic arts, not only sewing but also cooking, housekeeping, decorating, etc., *Fashion Service* was devoted entirely to giving current fashions with a key to their development.

Fashion Service prided itself on providing it's readers with reliable style information and the newest fashion forecasting. The publication wasn't just eye candy. The Institute stressed the importance of studying the fashions to benefit the sewer's understanding of dressmaking. To quote founder Mary Brooks Picken, "Once the principles of design...and of construction... are understood, beautiful garments will result. This publication comes to you as an aid to this desired goal. Read the text of every page and reason out the why of every illustration and description that your comprehension of designing and construction may be enlarged and your appreciation made more acute."

Today, these articles and illustrations give us a historically accurate view of what fashion really meant 100 years ago. Not only can we study these articles for an "of-the-time" style snapshot, but just as their students did, we can also learn to understand the principles of design and increase our sewing skills. In each issue, look for a collectible illustration in the back of the supplement!

Draping of Self-Trimmed Wrap

Cutting the Material.—In developing a coat, one must first make certain whether the material has an up and down, for the nap must run the same way in all parts of the coat, except possibly in certain trimming pieces. If the material has not a decided nap, the pieces should be arranged so that the nap will run up in both pieces, but in napped fabrics, it should run down. After the pieces are cut, they should be put together and notched, so that in the draping the nap in all the pieces will run in the same direction.

Developing the Muslin Model.—To drape a coat, you start with muslin, the coat material proving too heavy to hold in place satisfactorily. For a medium-size figure, provide two lengths of muslin, each one 27 inches wide. On the piece to be used for the front, turn under 4 to 7 inches on one lengthwise edge to serve as the facing and make the addition of a facing piece unnecessary.

Place this muslin up against a dress form or a figure, as shown in *1,* allowing it to extend to the left of the center front the distance desired for the overlap, and pin, as indicated, bringing it up on the shoulder smoothly and securely. Next, lift it just below the waist line so that the woof threads come straight around the figure between the waist and the hip line, and put a pin there, as in *2.* Lay a dart in the shoulder so that the underarm line is parallel with the warp threads, as in *3.*

With the dart pinned, mark the neck line, the armhole, which begins 5 to 7 inches above the low waist line, and the side-seam line, which is straight; then cut ¾ inch outside of these lines, as in *4.*

To develop the back, begin by folding the remaining piece of muslin through the center lengthwise and placing it up to the figure and pinning it, as in *5,* bringing it up well at the neck so as to insure ample height. Pin the side seams together, keeping the back edge as straight as that of the front, and mark for this seam as well as the armhole and the neck line. Then cut off the surplus material ¾ inch outside of the seam lines.

Now, as in *6,* pin the shoulder seam in a correct position square on top of the shoulder, easing a little fulness in the back piece to keep the coat in position, and cut. Then, as in *7,* turn under the armhole seam allowance to make sure the line effect is just what you desire.

For the sleeve, use a piece of muslin 4 inches narrower than the armhole measures on the seam line and 4 inches longer than your inside sleeve-length measure. Place this over the armhole of the coat with the center of the upper edge on the shoulder seam, and pin the front, as shown in *8,* and the back, as in *9,* extending the pins along the sleeve seam. Drop the arm down in trying this out to make sure that the sleeve is long enough on the top. Also shape the sleeve slightly at the bottom. Then, as in *10,* cut away the surplus material, slip the sleeve under the coat armhole, and pin to determine the effect.

For the collar, use a straight piece of material 3 inches wider than the shoulder length of the coat and twice as long as the neck measure from the folded front edge to the center back. Pin this around the neck, as shown, taking care to obtain a good neck line. Also, using a straight piece of muslin, pin this to the sleeve for the cuff.

Then, mark all lines accurately and unpin the model, preparatory to laying it on the coat material.

Cutting the Coat Material.—A little more care must be exercised in laying a muslin model out for cutting than in placing a pattern, for to keep it straight one must be guided by the warp and woof threads of the muslin rather than by lines or perforations. Place the muslin guide pattern as economically as you can, first noting whether there is an up and down either in figure or in nap. Tear on a crosswise thread whenever possible.

Construction and Fitting.—When the garment is cut out, lay it on a table smoothly, pin the side-seam and shoulder edges of the front pieces to those of the back, and baste with stitches ⅜ to ⅝ inch long. Also, baste up the sleeves. Baste the dart but do not stitch it. Stitch the seams, remove the bastings, and press the seams. Then, baste the sleeves in the armhole, and try the coat on.

Preparing and Applying the Lining.—Cut the lining exactly the size of the outside, but allow only ⅜-inch seams and subtract the depth of the hem and facings.

Stitch the lining up, sew in the sleeves, and press all seams. Then, place the right side of the lining to the right side of the coat, pinning the facing and hem edges together and making sure that the seam allowances are correctly and accurately placed. Baste the lining in place, and then turn the coat right side out and try it on. If the lining is correct, stitch it in place.

Finishing the Coat.—Press or steam the edges where the lining joins the coat. Bring the edges together at the neck and the bottom of the sleeves and baste them preparatory to joining the collar and cuffs. Tack the shoulder dart and the armhole seams of the lining and coat together inconspicuously with silk thread.

Make the collar and cuffs as directed in the special supplement and attach them, slip-stitching the lining in place at the neck line and the bottom of the sleeves. Apply the fasteners, and then brush and steam the coat.

Model 8 (a).—This costume coat of blue charmeen is made similar to Model 8, except that it has less center-front lap, is cut shorter, and has plaited self-trimming.

Model 8 (b).—For a beltless, full-length sports coat, this tan zibaline model cannot be excelled, with its crosswise stripes of alternate pile and flat weave.

1

2

3

4

5

6

7

8

9

8 (a)

8 (b)

10

Coats and Suits

Model 8A.—Claiming much prestige in the autumn mode is the tubular wrap-around coat, which, in its straight-hanging lines, goes even so far as to omit under-arm seams entirely. This omission is of particular merit in a coat of plaid or striped fabric as it permits an un-broken effect at the sides.

Of a utility type is this model of tan-and-brown plaid coating, which promises comfort and becomingness to a marked degree not only in its straight, loose lines, but also in the large convertible collar and the sleeves with armholes of generous size and even more width through the lower portion. A bias use of self-fabric makes an effective finish for the sleeve edges, and buttons covered with the darkest portion of the plaid stand out in pairs as a useful trimming for the collar, sleeves, and extended closing.

About 3¼ yards of 54-inch coating should prove sufficient to develop the model illustrated for a person of average size.

Model 8B.—By adopting the very newest note in three-piece suits, one is provided, also, with a separate coat that may be worn with other frocks, for the three-quarter length jacket fashioned on coat lines characterizes many of the three-piece costumes of recent development.

It is an elegant version of this mode that is shown here —black velvet with banding of squirrel at the lower edge of the jacket and the sleeves, and black silk and metallic silver embroidery completing a border effect along these same edges and likewise trimming the blouse portion and puff sleeves of the dress.

Flaring lines, fulness gathered in at the front neck line, and raglan sleeves are interesting details. The simple, roll collar secured with the tie ends of the fabric gains distinction by the contrast of its plainness with the trimming used elsewhere.

Crêpe satin in sapphire blue, which the French are promoting with fervor, forms the upper part of the dress and is repeated with excellent effect in the jacket lining. Egyptian red in place of the sapphire would provide another up-to-the-minute combination.

The design as illustrated requires 5¼ yards of 40-inch fabric, 2 yards of the same width for the blouse portion and jacket lining, and 3 yards of fur banding.

Model 8C.—Striped cloth in which a very warm tan predominates has in its own fabric the means of effective trimming for this smart tailored model. This is in the form of bands cut lengthwise of the material and applied around the lower part of the box coat and the close-fitting sleeves in contrast with the direction of the stripes in the suit. A small collar of yellow fox makes a becoming frame for the face and takes a bit from the general severity of the design.

The skirt may be made in simple, two-piece fashion with vertical slit pockets or as a wrap-around style.

In an average size, the suit requires about 3¼ yards of 54-inch fabric with 2¾ yards of 40-inch material for the jacket lining.

Model 8D.—Knee flounces, which have descended directly from the 1880 mode, are finding marked favor in coat as well as frock designs. Sometimes the flounce is in the form of a straight gathered or plaited section, but more often it is flared and applied without fulness, as in this model. Two rows of stitching placed above the joining line of the flounce and a like finish employed near the joining of the flare cuffs and the softly crushed collar make these lines more interesting and provide the only trimming of the design.

As you will observe, the coat hangs on comparatively straight lines to the knee flounce, but allows little freedom through the hip portion, which is the tendency of many modern styles.

A soft, downy woolen, a velour variation, in navy blue is the fabric of which it is fashioned.

Provide about 3⅝ yards of 54-inch fabric to develop the design for an average figure, with practically the same amount of 36-inch lining.

Model 8E.—If a suit is needed for only dress-up wear, no more delightful fabric than charmeen could be selected for it. The color and trimming, too, might be of an unusual nature, bay-leaf green, as in this model, being chosen, with collar of red squirrel and embroidery in self-tones bordering the jacket and flare cuffs.

There is much of style value in the lines of the jacket, with its straight, unbelted front, which extends into rippled sides, and its back, which evidences an abundance of ripples through the lower portion and has its waist-line fulness restrained by sash ends of the fabric that loop at the center.

The skirt borrows little in the form of trimming or style from the jacket, being merely of very plain design to set off more fetchingly the charm of the coat portion.

About 3½ yards of 54-inch fabric, 3½ yards of 36-inch lining material, and 15 skeins of floss are needed for the average figure.

Model 8F.—There is much of individuality and real beauty in this coat model, whose fabric is a velvety-napped woolen in phantom gray that, with luxurious softness, tones in with the grays of the squirrel-fur trimming.

Cut in two-piece fashion, the coat shows a slight tendency to blouse at a low waist line. A band of cordings accentuates the joining of the skirt portion, which features a circular panel secured along the side closing.

The sleeves are cut in wide bell effect in harmony with the flare of the panel, but otherwise the style is very straight as to line.

Average material requirements include 3½ yards of 54-inch material and 2½ yards of wide fur banding.

8 A

8 B

8 C

8 D

8 E

8 F

Look for a collectible print version at the end of this issue.

Misses' Costumes

Model 9.—Any more of charm and up-to-the-minute newness than are included in this model could hardly be combined in one frock. First, the fabric stands out with delectable emphasis—moiré in a blue somewhat brighter than navy. And then comes the design with its slender, unbelted, front portion, its long, tight sleeves smartly cuffed in double frills of very fine, white broadcloth edged with silver ribbon, and a broad, fence-like collar that repeats the fabric and trimming of the cuffs.

The back is provided with groups of plaits in panel effect restrained by a narrow belt of the fabric. Practically all the surplus width across the front is restrained at a low waist line by plaits or darts laid at each side, thus giving the model a princesse effect.

For the average miss, 4 yards of 40-inch material, ⅜ yard, 54 inches wide, for the collar and cuffs, and 2 yards of ribbon are needed.

Model 9A.—Slenderness of form and grace in the carriage of the figure are requisites for the successful adoption of the much-talked-about minaret tunic, but under these conditions, it is a most delightful and becoming fashion. Here, it is finished at the lower edge with several cordings, which emphasize its flaring lines, and is poised over a full-plaited foundation skirt. The youthful basque waist has its short kimono sleeves finished with cordings and is collared in an unusual manner with a scarf effect of white satin, whose ends loop at the center back. A motif embroidered just above the waist line in bright red beads stands out with pleasing emphasis against the black satin of which the dress is developed.

About 5 yards of 40-inch material, ½ yard for the collar, and 2 bunches of beads are required for the average miss.

Model 9B.—Jersey in coptic, which is a dark, brick red, makes up this very practical model, which is ideal for school or street wear. This is a simple, one-piece design, the front terminating in a tunic over a front foundation-skirt portion that is joined to a lining.

The collar and cuffs are of batiste of light ecru coloring, although they might be of broadcloth, if preferred.

Provide about 3 yards of jersey, and ½ yard of material, 36 inches wide, for the collar and cuffs.

Model 9C.—Here again is a wrap that depends entirely on its fabric for trimming and finds in such trimming an excellent substitute for fur. The design, which is of straight, simple cut except

for the circular flounce that finishes its lower edge, would be lovely in velvet of some bright, becoming color, such as turquoise blue, love-apple red, or burnished gold for evening wear, or in a darker color of this same fabric if the cape is desired for afternoons, also. The style would be more practical if made of broadcloth or a pile fabric.

You may make the collar of a series of vertical tucks placed as far apart as you desire them. To give the puffed effect, simply draw up the stitching of the tucks. A picot-edged frill of self-fabric finishes the lower edge.

For a cape of average size, provide 6 yards of material, 40 inches wide, and 3½ yards of lining.

Model 9D.—A unique trimming of crocheted silk in a red verging on fuchsia bands the side closing and lower edge of this blue-twill frock and, in bandings separated by rows of spice-colored wooden beads, forms the lower puffed portion of the sleeves.

The dress is a one-piece model slightly draped at the side-front waist line and held in across the back waist line with a broad sash of the material, which ties in a loop and ends at the side front.

About 2 yards of 54-inch fabric is needed for the average miss, the trimming requirements depending on your selection. Military braid or a figured fabric in bright colorings may be used instead of the crocheted banding.

Model 9E.—Roman-striped ribbon, wide novelty braid, or knitted banding used for the girdle and cuffs of this slender girlish design adds much to its effectiveness. And then, a facing of bright red applied to the narrow, right-side panel would be permissible with navy twill, provided the red harmonizes with the coloring of the girdle.

The model is really very simple in cut, having a full-length side closing accentuated by a wide tuck or facing and a few small tucks extending from the neck line.

Of material 54 inches wide, 2¾ yards is needed for the average miss, with 1⅝ yards of banding or braid.

Model 9F.—Given a combination of turquoise-blue taffeta, cream lace, and bright-colored nosegays, with a basque waist and an abundance of ruffles besides, and the result is sure to be a party or dance frock of winsome daintiness. Plaits stitched flat at each side front take care of the surplus waistline fulness of the basque portion and, with the nosegays, relieve the severity.

In the average size, this design requires 6 yards of taffeta and 1 yard of lace.

Fabric Trims Vie With Fancies

While ostrich and kindred feathery fancies are used as the chief garniture on models for formal wear, there is a distinct tendency toward the fabric trim of self- or contrasting material for street and general wear.

In Model 9, a cushion-brim, Breton sailor is developed out of black panne velvet, and a bias drape of the same velvet is drawn around the side of the semisoft, white-felt crown. This simple side-crown trim is completed with a one-loop-and-one-end bow applied flat on the brim at the left-side back.

Breadth is given to the right side of the tricorne in Model 9A by extending in a double-faced wing effect the side-crown scarf of uncut velvet ribbon.

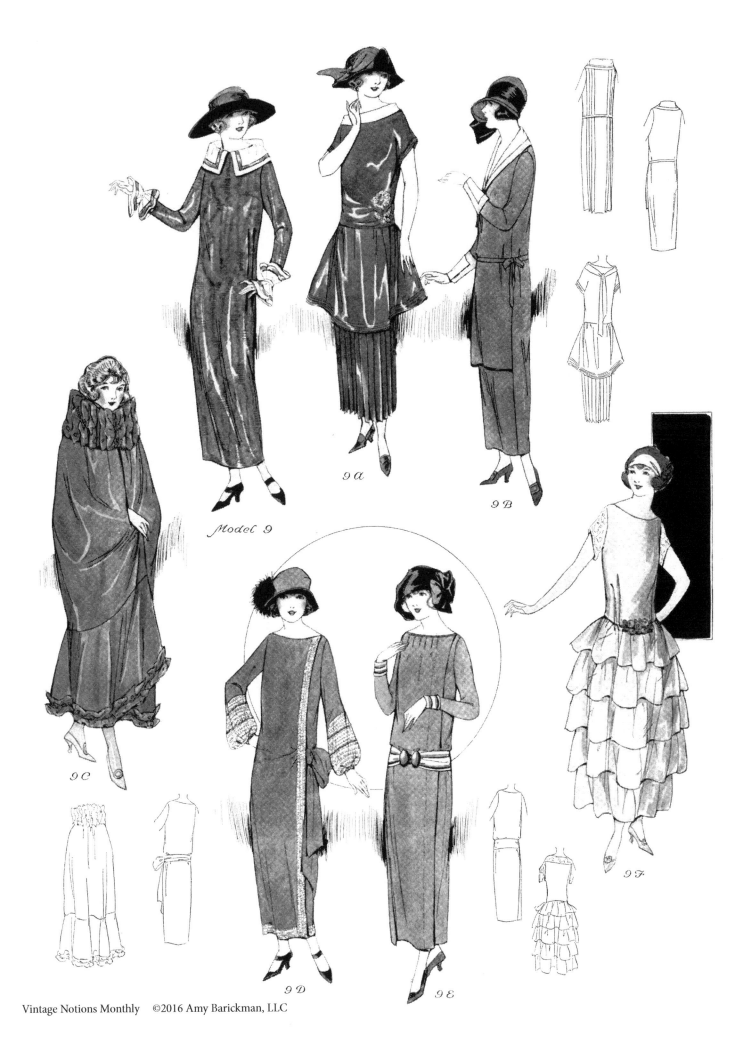

9A

9B

Model 9

9C

9D

9E

9F

Junior Fashions

Model 10.—Bright red as a trimming for navy provides such a youthful and an attractive contrast that there is small wonder it is the most popular choice for children's and misses' dresses. In the form of bead embroidery, it fashions long panel effects at each side front of this navy-twill model and trims the puff sleeves and lower edge of the little Eton effect across the back. A narrow collar of lace softens the finish at the neck line.

From the sketch of the back of this model, you will note that two plaits at each side back apparently extend from underneath the Eton effect for the remaining length of the dress. In developing the model, you may finish the lower edge of the Eton effect separately and apply the lower plaited portion to a waist lining, or you may secure the two together.

For the average girl of twelve years, 2½ yards of material, 54 inches wide, is needed. The simple embroidery design requires about 8 bunches of beads.

Model 10A.—Challis, a very soft, fine wool crêpe, crêpe de Chine, or Canton crêpe might be chosen for a tucked model such as this, which depends very greatly on the softness of its fabric for its desirability. The abundance of material and the crosswise lines make the style a particularly good one for the very slender girl.

Almond green, a soft medium blue, or a soft rose coloring would be especially attractive in the softer silks, but a darker and more practical color would probably be a better choice in challis or wool crêpe.

Of material 40 inches wide, about 4¼ yards is needed for the average girl of fourteen.

Model 10B.—Because of their adaptability to the growing girl's figure, raglan-sleeve coat models almost invariably find favor with discerning mothers, which must be one of the reasons why they receive considerable attention in new and varied interpretations each season. Set-in sleeves not only require more careful fitting in the making of the coat, but also appear at a disadvantage a second season if the width of the shoulders has increased, while a raglan sleeve molds itself readily to any increased size.

Made of a woody-brown pile fabric, this model relies on the use of bands of self-material cut either bias or straight and applied so that the nap runs in a different direction from that of the coat and thus appears of a different tone. Between these bands, rows of darning stitches worked in diagonal lines with wool of a slightly darker color complete an unusual border effect.

The shawl collar of generous proportions is tucked in practically solid effect across the sides and back and then extends in a wrap-around line to a low waist line, where a fastening is effected by narrow sash ends of the material.

For a girl of 14 years, a style developed in this manner requires from 2¾ to 3 yards of material 54 inches wide.

Model 10C.—Canton crêpe in Egyptian red, which is a very soft, slightly brown-tinged hue, makes up this graceful model, which would surely detract from even a suggestion of awkwardness that might otherwise be manifested at that troublesome "in-between" age. Self-color ribbon folded into a pointed insertion and secured between bound, slashed edges of the blouse provides a unique trimming for the front and the sleeves. The skirt, which is cut separate from the blouse, makes use of an abundance of material in its two broad tucks, and the sash, also, is unstinted as to size.

About 4½ yards of material, 40 inches wide, is needed for an average 14-year-old girl. Provide about 6 yards of ⅝-inch ribbon if you wish to use it as illustrated.

Model 10D.—This little design of Eton influence seems to have found its ideal accompaniment in the dark brown velveteen and lighter brown crêpe de Chine of which it is fashioned. The jacket portion could hardly be of simpler design and finish, the lower edge, fronts, and sleeves being bound with self-material and no decoration of any kind being called into use. But the guimpe and lower-sleeve portions of plaited crêpe de Chine aided by ribbons for the tie and wrist finishes supply the decorative touch that is needed.

The skirt, also, is of simple design, a straight, two-piece model having most of its waist-line fulness concentrated in soft plaits laid at the sides.

Average material requirements for a fourteen-year-old girl include 3 yards, 40 inches wide, for the jacket and skirt and 1½ yards of the same width for the guimpe and sleeve puffs, with 1½ yards of ribbon.

In making the dress, plan to attach the waist plaiting to a lining, extending this up under the jacket edge far enough to avoid having the joining show when the arms are lifted. You may secure the sleeve puffs directly to the lower edge of the jacket sleeves unless you prefer to attach them to a sleeve lining.

Model 10E.—That bustle tendencies can be charmingly adapted to frocks for the young girl is well demonstrated in this little model of soft taffeta in a medium blue that would serve equally as well for afternoon as for evening wear. The manner in which plaited ruffles are applied to the plain gathered skirt gives an apron and bustle effect of pleasing quaintness, which is further accentuated by the large fabric bow at the center back.

The waist is of a simple, drop-shoulder, blouse type with shoulder seams and has tiny puff sleeves formed of narrow straps of the material. A wisp of flesh-color chiffon is gathered into a tiny yoke that very interestingly follows the drooping line of the plaited skirt trimming.

In a ten-year-old size, this model requires about 3½ yards of material 36 inches wide. Not more than ⅛ yard of material is needed for the yoke portion.

Model 10

10 α

10 β

10 C

10 D

10 E

Children's Styles

Model 11.—Bands of braid in a dull blue that harmonizes very effectively with the warm henna coloring in which the wool crêpe for this frock was chosen, do much towards individualizing the kimono foundation of plain cut. Besides forming a narrow panel at the center front and a trimming band for the skirt, the braid covers the under-arm seams and the joining of the sleeves at a drop-shoulder line. A few scattered rosebuds embroidered in yarn complete the decoration.

An inverted plait in the back of the dress has the sole responsibility for its interest, with perhaps a little assistance from the collar of cream linen, which extends entirely across the back and separates at the center front.

In the ten-year-old size, a model such as this requires 1½ yards of 54-inch fabric, 6 yards of braid, and ¼ yard for the collar.

Model 11A.—Surely one has every reason in the world to be happy when one is prepared for the advent of the social season with a frock of such delightful nature as this little coral-colored taffeta model. It follows a scalloped path to unique distinction, the straight full skirt being bound in a soft-wave finish and trimmed with frayed-edge self-ruffles that follow the same curves. The little basque-like waist also effects a scalloped outline in the front, the space between the scallops revealing rows of shirring that confine the skirt fulness. Tiny puff sleeves, a white organdie collar, and a tie of soft blue ribbon make up the remainder of this fascinating style.

For a girl of eight years, provide 3 yards of 36-inch material and ¼ yard for the collar.

Model 11B.—Having fully as sophisticated an air as models designed for much more advanced years, this little coat should surely lend poise and satisfaction to a small wearer. The cloth is of the heavy camel's-hair variety in dark natural coloring, with brown stitching in lattice effect trimming the double-breasted front and lower edge of the sleeves.

Again, raglan sleeves are featured because of their practicability, and the scarf collar may have been introduced for the same reason, although first appeal comes through its smartness rather than its utility value.

You will need about 2 yards of material, 54 inches wide, to develop this model for a girl of eight. For the stitching, you may use heavy silk thread or, if you wish to do the work by hand, you may use wool floss applied in darning stitches.

Model 11C.—Just a few stitches of green wool as trimming, but how remarkably they touch up this little frock of navy twill. In the back, these stitches serve as stays for the edges of inverted plaits, which extend the full length of the dress in panel effect. And although they are not needed as stays in the front, they apparently serve this same purpose in the seam that joins the underlaid center-front portion and the tuck or dart edges at the shoulder. They are also effective in securing the burnished gold-color ribbon that, in double rows, bands the lower edge of the sleeve.

For a little maid of eight years, 1½ yards of 54-inch material should prove sufficient. In addition, 1¾ yards of ribbon and 2 small skeins of yarn are needed.

Model 11D.—If you are fond of crocheting, you will delight in developing a little dress such as this, which has all its seams and edges, except the neck line and skirt hem, finished with single-crochet edging. An open basket-weave woolen is its fabric, but wool or Japanese crêpe, also, would prove satisfactory.

As illustrated, the frock is of a colorful tan with crocheted edging and crocheted belt and tie of black, and cross-stitch trimming in red and fuchsia hues.

About 2½ yards of material, 36 inches wide, is needed for a girl of eight. For the crocheting, provide a ball of yarn and for the embroidery, two or three small skeins.

In making the dress, instead of stitching the seams, turn a hem along each seam edge and crochet around this; then crochet or whip these edges together with yarn.

Model 11E.—The vogue for plaid jersey was not long in spreading to children's wear. And small wonder, when it can find engaging designs such as this in which it is so effectively combined with a plain color. In this instance, the plaid is of medium and dark blue and the blouse portion, of a matching medium blue. A tan-and-brown plaid combined with plain tan would also be very desirable. Gingham, too, offers another possibility.

In making the dress, you may secure the full-plaited skirt directly to the blouse portion, using two rows of darker color stitching for this purpose. Cut the trimming band for the neck line and side opening as a fitted piece, letting this terminate underneath the pocket. Buttons and loops effect a fastening and provide an additional trimming feature.

In an eight-year size, this design requires about 1⅛ yards of plain material and 1½ yards of plaid material 54 inches wide.

Leather a New Juvenile Trim

The change in children's hat fashions from one fall season to another is so slight that the first glimpse does not always impress one, but on close observation you will find some special features that differentiate the new styles from the old. Sometimes it is the novel fabric used or the manner in which it is applied, or it may be the difference in the ribbon, its width, the length of the streamers, or possibly the absence of streamers, as in the modes for this season.

In Model 11, a very charming broad-at-the-sides poke made of black panne velvet becomes expressive by the use of leather for the binding, crown band, and hand-made poppy at the right side. Designs in water colors may be painted on the band and the flower when extra brightness is desired.

11 A

11 B

11 C

11 D

Model 11

11 E

Tiny~Tot Styles

Model 12.—The delicate beauty of tea-rose pink crêpe de Chine could hardly ask for a more desirable setting than in this frock for a wee miss, who also appears to have borrowed her coloring from a lovely rosebud. Quite in keeping with the delicacy of the fabric is the design, with its insertions of dainty, pin-tucked bands, its group of vertical pin tucks at each shoulder, and the double collar of cream Georgette picoted in scalloped outline and shaped to give a cape effect at the back.

At the side-closing of the collar, a bow of blue ribbon adds a French touch of character to the style.

About 2 yards of 40-inch material should prove sufficient for a six-year old, with ½ yard of the same width for the collar.

Model 12A.—This little play frock of sateen in a slightly grayed orange color should have a wonderful influence in brightening up a bleak winter day. And its making should prove almost as fascinating as its appearance, for it consists merely of a plain kimono foundation shaped up at the sides to reveal bloomers of matching fabric and trimmed with bands of novelty cotton braid of orange, green, and violet coloring.

Long puff sleeves may be added at a drop-shoulder line, as shown in the front view, or an abbreviated kimono sleeve maintained, as shown in the back view. With long sleeves, the design requires, for a four-year-old child, 2½ yards of material, 36 inches wide, and about 5½ yards of braid.

Model 12B.—When rompers are abandoned in favor of a very masculine suit such as this, it is only natural that one should prefer staid coloring as an indication of one's more sophisticated outlook on life. A very subdued green in a heavy cotton fabric used in the trouser and collar portions of the design and gray chambray for the blouse and frills should satisfy this exacting want and, at the same time, prove unusual and attractive. Brown and tan, green and tan, blue and tan, and blue and gray are other combinations that are certain to please.

For a four-year-old lad, 1 yard of the lighter color and 1¼ yards of the darker color, both in a 36-inch width, should prove sufficient.

Model 12C.—In planning a very best coat, one should be allowed to indulge in a color that is different from the average, perhaps a soft, rather light green, medium blue, or Egyptian red, a design that boasts a saucy flare, and fur of a soft, luxurious quality, though only a very small amount of this is permissible—in fact, just such a model as the one illustrated. Green, as it happens, is the color selection and beaver, the fur that edges the soft, high-rolled collar. The flare is provided by means of circular pieces set in at the sides and the joining covered with bands of the material.

In a six-year-old size, a model developed in this manner requires about 1¾ yards of material, 54 inches wide, and ¾ yard of narrow fur banding.

Model 12D.—Black military braid applied in the form of closely laid, flat loops accentuates the side closing of this little navy-twill frock and, in the form of a binding, finishes the neck line. The sleeves are of a dashing character—bright-red Canton crêpe—and add much to the novelty of the dress, but if you consider them a rather impracticable detail for the purpose you wish, you might make them of the twill also, cutting them in bell fashion and decorating their lower edge with a few flat loops of the braid. Do not fail to bring in a touch of bright color if you follow this latter suggestion, however, for just a couple of buckles of bright red or green added to the belt will relieve the darkness of the twill and braid trimming.

Of material, 54 inches wide, ⅞ yard should prove sufficient for a six-year-old girl. About 3½ yards of braid is needed and ½ yard of contrasting fabric for the sleeves.

Model 12E.—With a suit of wool jersey to fall back on, one may view approaching wintry weather with calm indifference for wool jersey is such a warm and comfortable fabric. The color of this little model, too, is very practical and satisfying, a pretty tan that should not show soil very readily. The blanket-stitching that edges the collar, slashed center-front opening, cuffs, and pockets is of brown wool.

For a four-year-old lad, 1⅜ yards of jersey and 2 small skeins of yarn will be required for this model.

Model 12F.—This is another little frock in which the seams and edges are finished with crocheting according to the suggestions given for Model 11D. The material suggestion is likewise the same, an open basket woolen, but the color is a bright henna and the trimming entirely in heavy, black, mercerized floss. Large henna-colored wooden beads finish the crocheted sash ends.

A six-year-old model requires about 1¾ yards of 36-inch material and 5 large skeins of floss.

Model 12G.—Tan taffeta has chosen a most unusual and delightful way of converting this demure little brown velveteen frock into a design of striking individuality. First, in applied strips, it bands the front of the dress in triple, vertical rows, and then, which is most interesting of all, fashions flower sprays with rolled edges to be secured over the lower ends of the bands. Taffeta bindings, too, prove a convenient and effective finish for the sleeves, neck, and slashed opening at the center back.

To develop the design, as illustrated, for a four-year-old child, provide 1½ yards of material, 40 inches wide, and ½ yard of taffeta for the trimming.

12 A

12 B

12 C

Model 12

12 D

12 E

12 F

12 G

Millinery Fashions

The same originality, the same rare smartness, that distinguished last season's hats, finds expression in the new modes for fall and winter. As predicted at the end of the summer season, China is exerting a marked influence over millinery fashions, not only in the shapes and colors, but in the fabrics as well, the richly embroidered and brocaded materials, which are prominent among the season's offerings, being redolent of the Far East.

The essence of the mid-Victorian, or Louis Philippe, lines is portrayed in the high crown and the small brim that rolls up on the left and down on the right side. It is evident that this snug-line hat will replace the turban of previous seasons. The medium-small mushroom is a popular shape, its soft crown assuming the new beret line akin to the tam of many sections. Soft or fitted are the new flared brims that take on the buccaneer, brigand, and jaunty picture lines.

Harmonizing in coloring with nature's present period of richness and harvest are the warm browns, not only golden brown but also the henna tones. Among the new reds are lacquer, garnet, mulberry, and wine reds, the last being devoid of any brownish tint and called dregs of wine. Considerable emphasis is given to palissandre of rosewood affiliation because it is sufficiently luminous to heighten the complexion pleasingly and combines well with the staple colors.

The fabrics, whether plain or fancy in weave, are truly elegant and in the development of models display remarkable beauty. They include chiffon, panne, and Lyons velvet, long-napped hatters' plush, felt, duvetyn, and faille silk, often covered with chenille and tinsel embroidery, and brocades in silk, metallic cloth, and velvet.

No longer content with facing and appliqué appearances, suède and leatherette are used to cover entire hats. Metallic and thread laces are in high favor, not only as constructing fabrics, but as trimming items.

Trimmings that bespeak the periods interpreted in the shapes are lavish beyond a doubt. Ostrich, which is paramount, fluffs, glycerines, or burns its flues, combines two or three treatments, or lets each play a lone rôle. Peacock has distinguished itself in novel fancies. Drenched maribou, striped hackle, and natural coque feathers are, after ostrich, the next plumage contenders for attention.

Ribbons show continued versatility and make bows, bands, and every other conceivable trimming touch. Flowers are to be had in rare, exotic, hand-made conceits, developed out of tinsel, suède, and shaded velvets in single blooms or in sprays. Here, at least, is one place where the ombré, or shaded effects of the previous season are retained in the making of the mode.

Model 13

13 α

13 B

13 C

13 D

*T*HE double brim of different sizes and usually made of contrasting fabrics, as shown in Model 13, is the new feature of greatest prominence this season. Gold metal cloth and lace are here used to cover the small inner brim, which droops a trifle at the sides, and palissandre Lyons velvet makes the flexible top brim and the two-piece bowl crown. A glycerined-ostrich blade trails gracefully across the turned-up back of the top brim and falls off at the right side.

Very simple, but with a charmingly decorative garniture is the capeline shown in Model 13A. Gray suède is the fabric employed for covering the brim and the tip of the crown. Tarragon-green velvet is draped softly around the coronet as a background for the suède motifs of various shapes that are appliquéd around the crown.

All black with a touch of brilliancy and a combination of brim lines is the hat theme emphasized in the model shown in 13B. As a foundation, a cloche with a helmet crown and an extra brim of the same size but rolling upward, is covered smooth with black panne velvet. From between the brims spreads a Breton-shaped wire brim covered plain with black thread lace, the edge finished with a narrow velvet binding. A rhinestone dagger pin thrust through the front provides a desirable note of brilliance.

Another indication that the double brim is a distinctive style feature is evident in the Model shown in 13C. Here, the brims follow the mid-Victorian line, rolling at the left and drooping at the right, where a low trimming arrangement of ostrich tips is attached. Two-tone brown velvet covers the brims plain, while the velvet covering of the round crown lies smoothly over the tip and is fulled into the head-size in four clusters of tiny plaits.

An extra brim flaring up and out in a broad-at-the-sides coronet effect from a close-fitting rolled brim, is an innovation in hatdom, but it promises to become popular, especially in hats for dressy occasions. In Model 13D, the close-fitting rolled brim and the soft, six-piece, sectional crown are made of bottle-green velvet. The semitransparent coronet of Chinese metallic brocade is fitted over a flaring coronet of wire, the edge being bound with velvet. The only ornamentation used is a small-sized butterfly of varicolored stones.

Hat Modes of Artistic Contour

Model 14.—Most noticeable is the prevalence of the mandarin and coolie types modified to suit modern needs. This Chinese influence brings about the use of large-patterned gold and silver brocade, especially displaying Oriental motifs studded with multi-colored beads.

Attractive and delightfully becoming is this version of the coolie cap. Gold metallic cloth, containing a blending of Oriental colors of odd greens, blues, and lacquer red, is used to make the six-piece sectional crown and fit plain the close mushroom and inverted-saucer combination brim.

From the beaded knob on the top of the peaked crown, a long silk-floss tassel falls over the right side of the brims and hangs below the waist line. For a variation of trimming, a twist of satin ribbon drawn between the brims and finished with a bow or a fancy double-pin ornament may be used.

For this model, 1¼ yards of 18-inch wide brocade is required.

Model 14A.—Lovely in every way is this tête de negre panne velvet hat, with its soft, bowl-top crown. The medium-large brim has an easy roll across the front, spreads out at its sides, and cuts off close to the crown at the back. The top and the under facing of the brim are fitted plain and a 1-inch binding is applied with a cord, top and bottom. Titian-color metal ribbon, side-plaited and formed into wing effects, is attached at the base of the crown on each side and extends beyond the brim edge.

To develop this model, 1¾ yards of panne velvet and 4 yards of No. 80 ribbon are needed.

Model 14B.—Unique handwork in a combination of colors and fabrics figures in the construction of this broad-at-the-sides, turban-effect model. Navy duvetyn is used for the crown and visor, while small velvet motifs in green, henna, royal blue, and beige cover the inverted coronet, or overhanging cuff, which spreads across the front.

To make the motifs, cut various-size pieces of panne and Lyons velvet, draw them up in a tight-shirred center, and finish with French knots and veins of metal thread; then turn the outer edge under with running-stitches of metal thread. Apply them to the coronet by stitching through the center and drawing the edges so that they shape into one another and form the unusual design shown. The inside of this coronet may be covered with duvetyn, after which it is attached to the visor turban.

The development of this hat affords an excellent opportunity to use up pieces of velvet that are left from fitted brims. To cover the turban, ½ yard of duvetyn is required.

Model 14C.—The decorative scheme featuring cunning handcraft and the soft drape of velvet that relieves the severeness of the upturned brim in this version of the buccaneer type, make this hat wearable with smart afternoon frocks or dressy tailleurs. Very soft yardage felt in beige makes the high, round, six-piece, sectional crown and the under facing of the flare brim. Cut-out motifs of felt in copper, cocoa, and tobacco, together with small disks in lacquer red and Chinese green, are appliquéd on the brim with a silk floss or fine chenille.

A long bias strip of tobacco panne velvet, 15 inches through the widest portion, is used for the soft top brim. Beginning at the extreme right side, sew one edge of the velvet around the outer edge of the brim; then turn this over the edge and allow it to form a soft roll. Drape it in soft plaits into the head-size, working the fulness toward the right side. At this point, twist the bias ends into a soft knotted effect that serves as a finish.

For the crown and under brim, ¾ yard of felt, and for the top brim, ¾ yard of velvet are required.

Model 14D.—An exponent of the tam vogue is here developed in wine color Lyons velvet and shaped over a flexible cuff brim that rolls high across the front and is placed on a small visor. The seam or joining of the circular tip and the side piece is hidden with a quilling of narrow metal ribbon. A rosette effect of hackle pads in pheasant coloring is attached rather low on the right side.

To develop this tam, 1½ yards of velvet and 9 yards of ribbon are required, and for trimming, from 4 to 6 hackle pads, according to the size of rosette desired.

Model 14E.—Possessing grace of brim line and dipping especially low on the right side, this picture poke is developed in terra cotta panne velvet. The rather high, slightly bell crown and the brim are fitted plain with the panne velvet. Then, beginning on the top edge and continuing to the head-size on the under facing, strips of Lyons velvet tubing are run around at 1-inch intervals. Three rows of this same tubing form the finish around the base of the crown. A long, full, fluffy plume sweeps across the abbreviated back brim and droops over the left shoulder.

To develop this model, 1½ yards of panne velvet, ⅝ yard of Lyons cut on the bias, and 10 yards of No. 1 cable cord are required.

Model 14F.—Palissandre scores again in this medium-large, broad-side shape having an edge flange slashed a trifle toward the back. The inner portion of the top brim and the softly draped high crown are of palissandre silver brocade, while the edge flange and under facing are of velvet in the same color. A fringed effect of glycerined ostrich in a matching color runs across the back brim, beginning on the top on the left side and ending on the under brim at the right. As a finishing touch, a double-head pin is used in the center front of the crown.

14 B

14 C

14 a

14 D

Model 14

14 E

14 F

14 G

14 H

The material required for this model includes 1 yard of metal brocade and ¾ yard of velvet.

Model 14G.—Following the line of the mid-Victorian period, the trotteur shape used in this model, with its high crown and snug brim that rolls on the left and dips on the right, is arresting considerable attention. Although this hat is covered severely plain with black, long-napped hatters' plush, velvet may be used and then the side crown may be applied in a soft draped effect. A spray of bronze, brown, and green coque feathers drooping off the brim at the right side provides another note that emphasizes the period.

When hatters' plush is used, 1 yard is sufficient, but for a soft draped crown 1¼ yards of velvet is required.

Model 14H.—The large, wide-at-the-sides brims, with a general attitude towards droopiness, bid fair to outdo their popularity of the past season, for in the loveliest of color combinations as well as in all black they are appearing in large numbers. Black, Chinese blue, and a touch of metal make up the color combination of this model.

The top brim is covered plain with black panne velvet. For the under facing, a bias strip of Chinese blue velvet, long enough to reach around the outer edge without stretching and wide enough to cover the widest portion of the brim, is side-plaited by machine. To apply this, draw out the plaits, sew plain around the outer edge, and then draw it into the head-size in plaits. Next, apply a 1-inch binding of black velvet on the edge.

The tip of the high, oval crown is covered plain with black velvet. Around the top edge of the crown cuff, strips of metal ribbon are sewed vertically for a distance of 2 inches, and the remaining portion is covered with a band of velvet. A cocarde of plaited Chinese blue velvet, finished in the center with a little of the metal ribbon, is applied flat on the brim at the left side.

For this model, provide 1 yard of the blue velvet, ¾ yard of black panne, and 3 yards of No. 5 metal ribbon.

$\mathcal{V}$ELVET, luxuriant and soft and rich in color, or satin, lustrous and new, is combined with beaded and embroidered Georgette in draped models. Moiré, brocade, and satin serve well in smart afternoon dresses as well as for those that are more tailored.

For evening wear, there are many alluring fabrics that are fashionable, chiffon velvets, the metallic tissues of gold and silver, gold and silver and colored brocades, all adaptable for smart and becoming dresses. Georgette and lace, chiffon and lace, and chiffon and brocade are all quite as distinctive, the silhouette, the color, and the smartness of effect determining the style value.

Soft, luxurious wraps of many descriptions are to be seen, and for these are used soft wool fabrics, fur, fur cloth, velvet, satin, and chiffon, velvet and satin making especially attractive wraps because of their sheen and draping possibilities. Evening wraps should always be lovely, soft, and becoming, possessing some claim to artistry to serve their purpose well.

Every hem line has its own mode of finish, keeping, however, in most instances, 8 to 10 inches from the floor. Every sleeve makes its own becoming stop and is trimmed in a way to harmonize with the neck-line finish. And this has a way all its own, from a narrow bit of fur to a lace bertha that droops waist deep in the back, or perhaps 'tis of fabric that surrounds the neck in great billows of soft loveliness.

Magic Pattern: Ribbon Accessories

▶▶▶ JADED DRESS or basic new one can be smartened with ribbon accessories. The collar and cuff set shown, for example, is made from 2 yds. of 3-in. picot-edge striped taffeta ribbon. Set requires six snap fasteners and is most reasonable in cost, considering the wear and smartness it can give you.

Pleated collar and cuff set: Cut your 2 yds. of ribbon into three pieces—two ½-yd. lengths for two cuffs, one 1-yd. length for the collar. Hem the six raw crosswise ends. Begin at one end to pleat. Make pleats ¼ in. deep and ½ in apart. Pin or baste, then press these. Stitch pleats in place ½ in. from edge on both collar and cuffs. Remove bastings. Sew two snap fasteners to each for closing, one at stitching line, other at other end. If desired, a narrow velvet ribbon may be tacked over stitching line and tied in a bow at each closing.

Sachet bows: A favored trick is to put sachet in your dress decorations. For example, this bow has a little piece of cotton wrapped around two teaspoonfuls of sachet and actually enclosed inside each end of top ribbon bow.

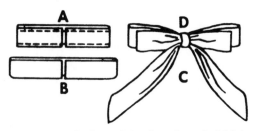

You need for this 1 yd. of 1½-in. striped taffeta ribbon and a safety pin about 1 in. long. Cut ribbon into four pieces, one 1 in., one 10 in. one 12 in., one 13 in. Fold 10-in. strip in half crosswise. Bring ends in to center and stitch edges, as shown at A. Insert sachet into each end of bow. Stitch across each end near center to hold bows.

Bring ends of 12-in. strip together as for 10-in. strip, as in B. Fasten ends of this together with stitches behind first bow. Fasten center of 13-in. strip behind this 12-in. strip, ends loose, as at C. With overcasting stitches draw raw edges of 1-in. strip together, thus holding securely all three pieces at center, as at D. Sew safety pin over joining of this 1-in. piece. Pull ends of 13-in. piece down and your bow is ready for wearing.

Ribbon clip-on: You need ¾ yd. of 3-in. ribbon, one button the size of a nickel, metal clip or safety pin. Cut ribbon so that you have a 2-in. piece and a 25-in. piece. Fold ribbon crosswise, bringing cut ends together. Stitch selvages on one side, as at E. Hem raw ends. Open out so that fold forms a point, as at F. Press. Fold hemmed end to wrong side 1 in. Gather from top down to within 4¾ in. of point. Draw gathers up tightly and sew, as at G. Cover button with 2-in. piece of ribbon and sew it on front directly in center of gathers. Sew clip behind gathers.

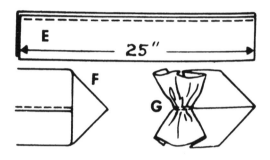

H: Buy 1¼ yds. of ribbon about 2¾ to 3 in. wide. Cut a length 4 in. longer than your neck measurement. Cut remainder into four even lengths. Fold neckband through center lengthwise and press. Lay pleats in one end of each of the four lengths and notch four ends. Stitch two of these to each end of neck band, as at H 1, concealing raw edges. Presto! You have a neckpiece that needs only a brooch to hold it in position. If desired, six 3-in. ribbon ends may be used, all worn to left side.

I: Cut off old neckline and sleeve finish of a tired dress. Face neckline and sleeves on wrong side with 1¾-in. true bias, turning ¼ in. on each edge for seams. Make a small buttonholelike opening, as in I 1, on each sleeve and front of neck. Finish these openings with buttonhole-stitch. Buy 2½ yds. of 1-in. ribbon (1¼ for neck, ⅝ for each sleeve). Run ribbon through casings, draw up to fit, finish with bows.

J: A tiny corsage and ¾ yd. of 3-in. ribbon makes this attractive neckline finish. Lay one or two pleats in neck part of ribbon and tack. Don't crease ends. Notch them as shown. Lap to fit. Sew on snap. Tack corsage to top lap as shown.

K: Belt worn out or lost? Buy waist measurement plus ¼ yd. of ribbon. Choose a ribbon 3 to 4 in. wide. Lay one or two length-wise folds in ribbon. Fold in ends and whip. Put around waist and hold in place with concealed pins or pin-on buttons.

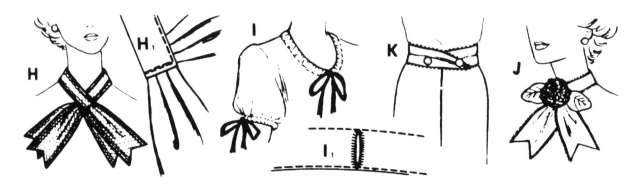

MARY BROOKS PICKEN

FOREWORD

The search for happiness carries us as individuals into the country, the streets, the parks, the churches, the homes, the theaters, and to books and magazines.

To know happiness we must appreciate beauty, and to appreciate beauty we must develop it within us.

A great degree of happiness may be had from a study of dress and its requisites, for, as we study, observe, and apply, our inner selves will awaken to the artistic side of dress, and once awakened will develop to such an extent as to give us understanding and appreciation.

This book comes to you not as a "Beauty Book," but as a study, and my earnest desire is that it will help you to see in dress beauty that you have not been able to find before.

An artist must know the principles of art to enjoy art or to make a success of it, and so must every woman know the principles of dress and enjoy dress to be successfully clothed.

Dress has such tremendous possibilities, such far-reaching effect, such power for individual success, that no woman can afford not to understand these principles as well as the niceties of dress.

This book does not attempt to exploit historic or ultra-fashionable dress, but to give as simply and directly as possible the fundamentals of dress, to give instruction in the whys and wherefores of individually becoming dress, and to help elevate dress and its requisites to the plane where dress will be appreciated and where it will become a happiness to women.

I wish to express my appreciation to the editor, Mr. G. L. Weinss, for his splendid and untiring assistance.

Mary Brooks Picken

Originally published in *The Secrests of Distinctive Dress, 1918*

THE SECRETS OF DISTINCTIVE DRESS

CHAPTER I

YOUR INDIVIDUALITY

YOUR DISTINCTIVE CHARACTERISTICS—KEYNOTE TO DISTINCTIVE DRESS—OVERCOMING DAME FASHION'S UNREASONABLENESS—SELF-ANALYSIS.

Personality is the outward expression of that indefinable quality known as "individuality." Personality we can develop—can really create. How? By making it express in the fullest sense our highest and best aspirations.

Personality carries great responsibilities, because we expect it to represent us as individuals. We should therefore clothe our personality with honest thoughts, high ideals, and lofty purposes; and to enable it to forge ahead—to permit us to reach the pinnacles of our aspirations—we should clothe its dwelling place—our body—with agreeable and proper raiment, raiment that will not hamper it but stimulate it to guide

Artcraft Pictures   Photo by Victor Georg

ELSIE FERGUSON

Whose personal charm is enhanced by her delightful application of
superior dress knowledge

our pursuits, to make friends and success for us.

Your individual characteristics should dominate you, your ideas, your attitude toward life and toward those with whom you come in contact.

Your clothes help you to express your innermost thoughts, your kindliness, your good feeling toward all about you. This should be sufficient reason for knowing your good and bad points and understanding yourself well enough to bring out the charm you possess or to cultivate charm if you feel that you lack this invaluable quality.

You should never be satisfied to be a nonentity in intellect, in understanding, or in friendship. You should express your personality in these things, and, in doing this, one of the greatest aids is dressing yourself appropriately, becomingly, and with individuality.

Sometimes, women misinterpret the worthwhileness of individuality in attire and resort to freakish costuming. We may be grateful for the infrequency of such mistakes, for there are few women—yes, very few—who do not desire to dress in the most becoming way possible, and who will not, with aid and encouragement, persevere until capable of dressing in a distinctive, beautiful way.

It is my desire in this book to give you authentic and definite information that will enable you to distinguish between what is worth while and what is not, and so help you to select such materials, colors, and designs for your garments that they will harmonize with your individuality and environment.

The experience of designers and creators of wearing apparel has demonstrated that harmonious dress is simply the result of a proper knowledge of color, basic motifs of design, the kind of fabric to employ for a given purpose, and the lines of the human figure. Therefore, instead of being perplexing, harmonious dress —distinctive dress—is simply the result of good judgment used in selecting colors and fabrics and choosing and adapting styles that, in motifs of design, suit the lines and proportions of your figure.

To be clothed in garments that in every way bring out your best points and in no way emphasize any of your defects should be your aim. There are comparatively few women who can afford to be richly dressed; yet, no woman, no matter what her station in life may be, can afford to be shabbily dressed.

Next to your ability—and some claim before it—comes your personal appearance.

Your clothes are your visiting cards—your cards of admission, so to speak—and you cannot afford to be tabooed because of being untidy or dressed unbecomingly.

A really well-dressed woman is never conspicuous nor uncomfortable no matter where she may be. To be well dressed, however, does not necessarily mean that you must be extravagantly dressed; it does mean, though, that you must understand dress harmony—how to adapt prevailing styles to harmonize with your personality and to conform to it.

KEYNOTE TO DISTINCTIVE DRESS

The keynote to distinctive dress is to *know yourself*—your good points, as well as your shortcomings. Every little part of your personality has a direct bearing on what you may wear to the best advantage.

Your figure controls the lines of your garments; your complexion, and even your temperament, the color; and your occupation or station in life, the fabric. Yet, associated with all these is the dominant question of fashion.

It is not wise for any woman to let thoughts of fashion sway her entirely; yet, since clothes are a very important factor and they, in turn, are regulated by style tendencies, it would be unwise to overlook style conditions.

Style has the power of adding much to the appearance of a garment if just a little thought is given to it. Thus, to illustrate my point, suppose we consider a dress or a suit that is, say, only a year old. When new, it was considered very smart; yet in only one short year it seems to have lost the charm it had for us— is no longer satisfactory.

Why this change?

The fabric may be almost as good as when the garment was new, the color is practically the same, and it fits just as well as ever. What else then can it be if it is not the change in fashion—our conception of new lines—that makes the costume appear less attractive to us?

None of your outer garments should be regarded as a meaningless covering; rather, they should be considered as a part of you.

Garments have the power of magnifying physical imperfections—to make one look conspicuous, undignified, and even absurd; also, they have the power to emphasize good points and make one feel comfortable and always at ease. Therefore, by close and careful study, you should endeavor to find out what is most beautiful in yourself, and then set about to express this beauty as cautiously, as carefully, and as appropriately as you can.

Garments of harmonious colorings that are carefully constructed will always tend to enhance one's appearance, and an appropriate costume correctly designed will lend grace to the figure and an ease that aids in bringing out one's individuality.

Whatever your station in life may be, therefore, it is really your duty to study the lines of your face and your figure. Then you should give every detail, from the arrangement of your hair to the condition of your shoes, intelligent thought and careful attention. By heeding such advice you will be able to select styles that are practical and appropriate and yet becoming.

OVERCOMING DAME FASHION'S UNREASONABLENESS

To emphasize the necessity for a wise selection of wearing apparel, I cannot refrain from mentioning that many women seem to be powerless to overcome the unreasonableness of Dame Fashion.

Every season brings forth new colors and new lines; and many women in their endeavor to be, as they think, fashionable, hasten to adopt these new colorings and new lines without giving any thought as to whether or not they suit their particular type.

To be fashionable does not mean that you should adopt every new fad just as it is given out; rather, it means that you should intelligently readjust the prevailing style so that it will conform to the lines of your face and your figure.

After you give due consideration to dress that is becoming, in no case can you afford to overlook its appropriateness. The proper dress, you will find, is the one that agrees with your station in life and with the work that is to be done in it or the purpose for which it is intended. Successful business women, society women, and home women appreciate the necessity of wearing appropriate, becoming costumes in order to be able to cope with all duties that confront them.

Besides style and coloring, therefore, the fabric of your garments must receive consideration. The fabrics you select for your dress should invariably be those best suited to your needs, as well as to the season of the year, the time of day in which the garment is to be worn, and the character of the garment.

A knowledge of the things that lead to harmonious dress is valuable to every one. It aids in the proper selection of dress, serves to give new courage, new interest, and oftentimes new hope to those who realize its possibilities, and arouses in every woman a love for all that is beautiful, right, and elevating.

All who strive to follow the details that bring about dress harmony will be well repaid, for they will experience the satisfaction of having serviceable, graceful garments that will be healthful, comfortable, stylish, splendid on occasions, and, best of all, garments that will add to a woman's charms rather than detract from them.

SELF-ANALYSIS

Analyze the efforts that have been made to produce a standardized dress for woman, and you will find that there is a legitimate reason for this agitation. Certain women who have become more or less efficient in their dress, and who do not look to the individual becomingness of dress so much as to its service, are trying to persuade women to be more efficient in buying and wearing their clothes.

The dominant question in many minds is, "Will standardized dress make women efficient with regard to dress?" My opinion is to the contrary. I do believe that *individual dress* will bring about efficiency—yes, more than efficiency—because it will give us beautifully and correctly dressed women, a combination very much to be desired.

The woman who is at home all morning and probably goes shopping once or twice a week or to some charity meeting or church gathering and the woman who goes to business every morning do not have the same clothes requirements. The woman who has a limousine to take her about does not have the same clothes requirements as the woman who must walk. The woman who goes to elaborate dinner parties and other evening affairs does not have the same clothes requirements as the woman who has a simple dinner at home with her family. The woman who plays golf or tennis and drives her own car does not have the same clothes requirements as the woman who has neither the time nor the inclination to engage in such sports or pleasures.

It would be difficult to put down all types of women and their various clothes requirements, but I hope I have named enough to make clear the necessity for self-analysis. It is for you to decide what kind of clothes you must wear to be becomingly and fittingly dressed. You must realize that if you are going out to business you should not dress as you would if you were going to a church gathering; nor should you, if you are going to an elaborate dinner party, wear a shirtwaist and skirt, as you may be privileged to do at a

simple home dinner with your own family or with intimate friends.

It is for you to decide, too, how long a suit or a dress must serve you, whether you must spend your clothes money for a tailored suit, two afternoon dresses, and two evening dresses, or whether you can spend the full amount on a tailored suit and one semi-evening dress that may be used for the afternoon functions that you may attend.

The same analysis should be made in the matter of your hats, shoes, gloves, and all dress accessories, so that you can divide your dress allowance according to your individual needs, and at the same time be sure that you have adhered strictly to the rule of providing becoming and proper clothes.

It is better to have one dress or one suit that is becoming and the best your funds can possibly buy than to have two or three garments that might appear cheap and shabby.

To my mind, an old garment of good material that is becoming is much better than a new garment that looks cheap. Do not discard clothes of beautiful materials and good workmanship that are right for you simply because you feel that they are not up to the fashion of the moment. It is better not to procure garments so extreme that they will go out

of fashion before the required service is had from them. Buy good materials, make them up as appropriately and as attractively as you can, and then be a law unto yourself regarding the amount of wear you get out of them.

As you read the instructions in this book, have your own needs constantly before you, not the needs of your neighbor. Remember that becoming dress fitting to *your needs* is the kind of dress for *you.* Keep this thought constantly before you, and you are bound to be benefited. You will be able to dress more attractively and to wear clothes that suit your individuality at less cost; besides, clothes will then mean more to you than ever before.

There are other considerations regarding your individual dress. How much time and thought can you afford to give to your clothes? How much time can you spend in putting on and taking off your clothes? Few women consider these points. They see a dress that is pretty; they like it. But they do not consider how long it is going to take them to put it on and take it off, whether they can afford, in the morning, to take the time required to put such a dress on, provided they must go out to business. Then, too, they do not take into consideration whether it is going to give the service that they require of a dress.

A very prominent American woman writes definitely about the length of time that women give to putting on and taking off their clothes. She says that if women are to succeed in business, they must throw off the shackles of dress. They should so systematize their clothes that they can get into and out of them as quickly as a man gets into and out of his. If men in offices are called on to go into the street quickly, they can don a hat and coat and be properly dressed. In many instances, if a woman is going to town shopping, it takes her an hour and a half to get ready to go out; and when she returns she must change, requiring from twenty minutes to half an hour to do this.

Such conditions as I have mentioned cause me to be an enthusiastic advocate of having every woman make a self-analysis, anticipate her clothes needs, and determine upon the length of time and the amount of money she can afford to spend on her wardrobe. When every woman appreciates what individual dress will mean to her personally, and then puts her appreciation into practice, women will be more beautifully and distinctively dressed than ever before and fully satisfied that not half the amount of money or time will be spent as when they endeavored to live up to the standard of dress set by their neighbors.

Photo by Charlotte Fairchild

ETHEL BARRYMORE

A definitely charming personality—a type whose clothes must ever
exemplify perfection

Vintage Notions Monthly continues to share the work of Mary Brooks Picken and the Woman's Institute which inspired my book *Vintage Notions*. Although the Institute was founded 100 years ago, the treasure trove of lessons and stories are still relevant today and offer a blueprint for living a contented life.

If you enjoyed this issue of *Vintage Notions Monthly*, visit AmyBarickman.com for more of my curated collection of vintage content including patterns and books for needle and thread, inspiring fabric and textiles & free vintage art every Friday. Be sure to tune in to *Vintage Notions* episodes for a guided tour through my collection of sewing and fashion history, as well as modern projects inspired by my extensive library.

Vintage Notions Monthly, Volume 1, Issue 12 (VN0112)

Made in the USA
Lexington, KY
10 November 2017